Me, Myself, and I

Memoirs of Elaine Andrus Watts

First Edition

Biographical Publishing Company
Prospect, Connecticut

Me, Myself, and I

First Edition

Published by:

Biographical Publishing Company
95 Sycamore Drive
Prospect, CT 06712-1493

Phone: 203-758-3661   Fax: 253-793-2618
e-mail: biopub@aol.com

All rights reserved. No part of this book may be reproduced or transmitted in any form or by any means, electronic or mechanical, including photocopying, recording, or by any information storage or retrieval system without the written permission of the author, except for the inclusion of brief quotations in a review.

Copyright © 2012 by Elaine Andrus Watts
First Printing 2012

PRINTED IN THE UNITED STATES OF AMERICA

Publisher's Cataloging-in-Publication Data

Watts, Elaine Andrus.
Me, Myself, and I / by Elaine Andrus Watts.
1st ed.
p. cm.
ISBN 1929882696 (alk. Paper)
13-Digit ISBN 9781929882694
1. Title. 2. Memoir. 3. Short stories. 4. Poems. 5. Christian life. 6. Family life.
Dewey Decimal Classifications: 920 – Biography
Library of Congress Control Number: 2011919170

INDEX

My Friend Jimmy
Playing "Dress-Up"
My Tire Swing
Our Dog, Old Ned
Making Mud Pies
When My Love For Pipe Organs Began
A First Grade Student
Afraid of Cows
I Am Honest
I Like To Sing
Perfect Attendance In First Grade
California, Here We Come
When My Love For Jesus Began
The Hammock. . . A Swinging Couch
Cod Liver Oil
I Can Play The Piano
The Stocking Cap
I Remember When. . .
I Liked Mondays
Beware of Electricity
My Heaven On Earth
Invited Guest
Summer Fun
Riding My Bike
My Doll House
Making A Big Playhouse
Things I Did For Fun

I Am An Architect
My Horse
Harvesting The Hay
Special Remembrances
Our Farm
I Can Drive
Teenage Triumph
Am I A Sneak or What?
A Few Of My Most Embarrassing Moments
Jobs, Jobs, And More Jobs
The Professional Music World
"Best" Neighbor
An Answer From Heaven
Raising Children
Food...Food...Food
Catholic Church Organist
A Few Early School Teaching Experiences
Writing Poems
Some Of Our Pets
Fun Times With Children And Grandchildren
Poems From My Heart
Community Service
A Treasured Compliment
I Wrote a Book
Directing The Master Singers
Survival Trip To Glacier National Park
Pearl Harbor
Music
A Few Public School Substitute Teaching Experiences
My Last Day Being a Public School Substitute Teacher

PREFACE

I've enjoyed remembering many incidents of my life. I hope, as you read them, you will recall events of your life. Perhaps you will want to share them too.

MY FRIEND JIMMY

Jimmy James comes to visit. We are both five years old. We ride my little green tricycle. I ride it in circles as fast as I can go. When it's Jimmy's turn, he rides fast in circles too.

We get tired of riding and sit on the grass by Old Ned, our big black dog. He thumps his tail. His long, red tongue hangs out. He pants because it is hot.

We sit awhile, petting Old Ned. Then we go look for the three kittens. They take naps under the long porch by the kitchen door. I call "kitty, kitty". Their heads peek out. When they see us, they dart under the porch again.

Jimmy's parents come to tell him they are ready to leave. Now I can't play with Jimmy any more. But they will come another day.

I climb back on my tricycle. I go 'round and 'round in circles as Jimmy and his parents drive away.

PLAYING "DRESS-UP"

A grape arbor is close to our house. It is shady and cool in the summer. My sister and I play "dress-up" in the grape arbor. We pretend that we are famous movie stars. Our new names are Joan and Jean.

Mother's high heeled shoes are on our feet. Long, lacy white curtains are draped around our shoulders. The curtains are evening dresses. We carry big purses.

Our lips and cheeks are painted with bright red lipstick. We hold our heads up high. Our boyfriends are coming to take us on a date.

MY TIRE SWING

'Round and 'round I twist in my tire swing. The ropes have no more room to twist. I lift my legs off the ground and WHEE . . . the swing unwinds. It goes fast.

I hold my head down. I hope it won't fly off. Finally the swing stops. My feet touch the ground again. I look up. The sky is whirling 'round and 'round.

I take a big breath.

That was fun! I do it again.

OUR DOG, OLD NED

Old Ned has a long, red tongue. His ears feel silky and his black coat looks shiny. He wags his tail when he sees me.

When evening comes, the cows need to be milked. We point to the pasture and say, "Good dog! Go bring the cows home."

Old Ned runs to the cows, circles around them, then slowly they all come to the corral.

The milk is strained into two big metal cans. They are placed on a little red wagon. Old Ned sits on the wagon behind the cans.

His two back legs surround one can. His front legs lay on the handles of the can.

Old Ned likes to ride on the wagon. He grins, showing his teeth. His red tongue hangs out.

I love Old Ned.

MAKING MUD PIES

Ireta lives across the road. She comes to play with me. With old spoons, we stir up dirt and water in two tin cans. We are making mud pies.

We pour little mounds of mud on the edge of the big porch. We decorate our pies with short pieces of grass, small leaves, and little rocks. Now they are ready to bake in the sun.

Ireta goes home. It is time for me to eat. Then I will take a nap.

I take off my gray coveralls and climb into bed. When I wake up I go outside again.

Our mud pies are done.

WHEN MY LOVE OF PIPE ORGANS BEGAN

We went on a trip to Hyrum, Utah, close to the university town, Logan. My mother's sister Nellie, brother Alma and her cousin Esther lived there. My sister Nyal and I went to the children's weekly Primary meeting with our cousins. I can still see myself standing in the doorway of the church listening to the pipe organ play the first song, "Called To Serve." I was five years old. I had never consciously heard a pipe organ. At that moment I fell in love with pipe organs. My sister, finding I was not following her, came back and jerked me along to get to our seat before the opening prayer. I couldn't keep from looking at the stained glass windows with the sun shining through illuminating the pictures. It was like being in heaven.

Some of the exhilarating moments of my life have been playing the pipe organ. With all your physical body (including your feet) and mind involved, there is no way to describe another dimension you feel while playing a J. S.

Bach "Prelude and Fugue," for instance, or some other masterwork.

One afternoon I waited in the back of the basement Primary room of our white rock church for my mother to finish with her Primary presidency meeting. I heard her say, "Elaine can be the Primary organist; she is taking piano lessons."

The meeting closed with prayer and my mother called me to come up. She said to me, "You can be our organist." (The present organist was moving.) I remember the chorister giving me a skeptical look, and then she picked out three songs to sing the next week.

I had recently turned eleven years old. I had taken piano lessons less than one year from a man teacher who drove around the farm communities giving lessons in people's homes. I was afraid of him. He had black greasy hair and reeked of cigarette smoke which sickened me.

I did not know how to read notes, except Middle C. Actually I played the pieces by ear and by following the many finger numbers on the notes. I had heard them played by three of my siblings, quite some time before this. Hopefully I would start on the right note in relation to Middle C, then play the tunes already in my memory. One time the teacher said to me, "Alright, now play it again and this time in the right key." (I didn't realize I hadn't.) I don't remember him explaining anything to me; he only listened, then assigned a few pages for the next week. I was always glad to be done.

In my day, children were seen but not heard; at least it was so in my family. It never occurred to me to protest being the Primary organist. I must have had an inner feeling that if I tried I could do it somehow. I think this approach to many challenges in my life has seen me through them without complaints or whining. I really felt indifferent about my ability to play the piano and there was no conscious pressure or competition. Right at this same time, because of World War II, my teacher quit teaching to farm full time in order to avoid the Draft. He was married and had five children. I bravely began trying to learn the Primary songs. A few days later, my oldest sister Beth came home for the weekend from her nurse training in Idaho Falls. She heard me practicing (crucifying) the songs and asked me what I was doing. I said, "I'm the new Primary organist. I have to learn these songs for next Wednesday."

She said, "I'd better help you." She explained the skips and steps of the music staff, time signatures, etc. It was fascinating to me. I began reading notes, not just fingering numbers. The Primary music didn't have any fingering. It was all like a revelation for me. Now I'm grateful she would take her time to help me. A big thanks also goes to my Mom for her confidence in me, though it was not based in reality.

That was only the beginning. Playing the little pump organ was a challenge. I had to keep my feet pumping the air while pushing the volume panels with my thighs. I think Heaven helped my organ technique, for I had been given no instruction.

From then on I read music like I was gobbling up ice cream and cake. It was fun! I could do it! Eventually I became the best sight reader in the area, and people came to me from all over to play for their vocal and instrumental performances.

At age thirteen or fourteen I began playing the pump organ for the main Sacrament meeting on Sundays. I still had not had any organ lessons. All this was the beginning of being a church organist for sixty years. The reason I finally had to stop playing the organ was because of arthritis in my hands. A sad trial for me.

Finally, the summer I was sixteen, I was privileged to take some organ lessons at Ricks College. I would drive to

Rexburg alone two or three times a week. I practiced three hours at a time on the college practice pipe organ. I loved learning to play with proper organ technique, and I was more than willing to pay the price with my effort.

Did I come from a musical family? Not really. My Dad loved the church hymns and led the singing in our church. Actually he just waved the stick. He knew nothing about beating the correct time signatures or other aspects of conducting. Mom had a beautiful alto voice but was shy about using it. We heard country music on the radio, the hymns and primary songs at church and the John Thompson Piano Course piano books. That was it. There was a big phonograph upstairs in my bedroom with a *few* scratchy old records. One that I loved was of Caruso, the world famous tenor. I think the love of Classical music came with me from heaven, for except for this record, I never heard classical music in my home. When in my mid teens, I attended productions of the *Messiah* with soloists from Salt Lake City and Mischa Elman, the world famous violinist, at the Rexburg Tabernacle. They hooked me on great music forever.

A FIRST GRADE STUDENT

Before I started first grade, my big sister, Beth, taught me to write all the letters of the alphabet. And I learned to write all the numbers up to twenty. I practiced on a little blackboard using chalk and an eraser. It was fun. I was a good student for my sister.

At school, Mrs. Smith was my teacher. She was kind. I liked her. All the first and second graders of our country school in Idaho were in Mrs. Smith's room. We learned to read by the phonics system. Our readers had stories about Dick and Jane. "See Dick. See Dick run. See Jane. See

Jane run." There were pretty pictures of Dick and Jane.

I liked to read. I still like to read. Books can take me places and give me adventures.

AFRAID OF COWS

I liked being a first grader in school. But after school, when it was time to walk home alone, I felt afraid. Cows often grazed in the deep, grassy borrow pits on both sides of the two-lane paved highway. I was afraid of the cows.

I didn't tell anyone that I was afraid. Did I think no one would care? Would I be laughed at? I don't remember what I thought or why I didn't tell anyone.

On days that cows were grazing in the borrow pits, I crawled through the barbed wire fences and walked in the pastures. After passing the cows a safe distance, I crawled back through the fences and walked on the gravel shoulder beside the paved highway.

Many years later, my son asked me why I had been afraid of cows.

I answered, "I don't know why."

I still don't know why.

I AM HONEST

My first grade teacher, Mrs. Smith, gave each student in our class a toothbrush and a chart. She showed us how to mark an X on the days we remembered to brush our teeth. If we forgot to brush, the little square on the chart must not have any mark in it. Students who had an X in every square to show they had brushed their teeth every day for two weeks, would be given a prize. We all wanted a prize.

I took my tooth brush home and hung the chart on the wall. I didn't mind brushing my teeth. I liked marking the X on the chart. I wanted to win a prize.

The day came to take the chart back to school. One of my parents must sign their name that I had brushed my teeth on the days that were marked with an X. But "Oh." One of the days did not have an X. I had forgotten to brush my teeth that day.

I gave the chart to my father. "I only forgot one time. Can I mark an X anyway?" I begged. "I remembered all the other days."

My father looked at me and said, "But that wouldn't be honest, would it?"

I hung my head, slowly shaking it back and forth, back and forth. I knew it wouldn't be honest.

At school, I gave the teacher my chart. All the days but one were marked with an X. Mrs. Smith was proud that we all remembered to brush our teeth most of the days. She gave every student a prize. I felt happy that I was honest.

I LIKE TO SING

Do you like to sing? In first grade, I sang duets with another first grader, Kay Beck. He sang the harmony and I sang the melody. The songs we liked to sing were "Days of Summer Glory," "Little Green Valley," and "Silver Haired Daddy of Mine."

We sang on programs. One time we won a prize at a Major Bowes program held at another community's church.

My family tells me that when I was a year old baby, I would blow on a mouth organ I held up to my mouth. I did it over and over again. I must have liked hearing the musical sounds.

When I taught grade school, I sat on a high stool at the piano and looked at the students while I played for them to sing. I only looked at the music if I didn't know the words. I could make up the piano accompaniment if I knew the tune in my head. Students would ask me how I could do that.

I think I learned about music in heaven before I was born. Songs and singing make me feel happy.

PERFECT ATTENDANCE IN FIRST GRADE

My teacher, Mrs. Smith, gave me a little book, <u>The Ugly Duckling</u>, for my perfect attendance in first grade. I didn't miss a single day of school that year.

I loved the pretty, colored pictures in the book. I felt sad about the troubles of the duckling. But the story has a happy ending. The ugly duckling turns into a beautiful swan.

Mrs. Smith gave me a necklace and bracelet set too. I had never had anything so pretty. I felt special when I wore the necklace and bracelet.

I've always liked going to school.

CALIFORNIA, HERE WE COME

The summer I was seven years old, our family (Mom, Dad and five kids) went to California. Dad's insurance partner took his wife and daughter, who was my age, in their car.

Here are some of the things I remember about that trip: seeing Grand Canyon and Bryce Canyon, a lady smoking in Reno, Nevada – I just stood and stared, taking a dip at the cold San Francisco beach, the World's Fair at

San Francisco, the Golden Gate and San Francisco Bay bridges, the zoo in San Francisco where Dad reached in and pulled the lion's tail and touring the battleship U.S.S. Arizona which was docked at the Los Angeles harbor. I remember a sailor teasing me, and I liked it. The ship was later sunk at the Pearl Harbor attack December 7, 1941. Hearing that, I felt sad.

Best of all was the fun house at a Los Angeles beach. I don't think anyone was watching me very well. I kept going into the huge barrel that never stopped turning and having to be pulled out over and over again by the attendant. Also, I loved driving the little cars and going down on the big slippery slides. If you didn't keep the gunny sack wrapped around your legs, you got burned. What fun it all was!

I remember a family that lived in Los Angeles where we stayed a few nights. The mother was the sister of Dad's partner. Another summer this family came on vacation to Idaho. We had more fun times with them – watermelon busts at the sand hills and a swimming party at Heise Hot Springs.

WHEN MY LOVE FOR JESUS BEGAN

"Mr. and Mrs. Andrus," said the doctor. "Your little girl's low-grade fever means she could have rheumatic fever, caused by a bacteria. Sulfa drugs are not effective. I wish we had a drug to take care of it. I can hear a heart murmur; a valve is not opening and closing properly. Complete bed rest will help her body's natural healing processes and prevent permanent damage to her heart. With good care, she can probably have a normal life."

In 1940, before my eighth birthday in late March, I had developed a low grade fever that did not go away. I couldn't finish the second grade at the little country school in Idaho.

I was put to bed and told not to sit up or get up. Being an obedient child, I did not whine or complain those six months. I had few toys to play with, and I was not allowed to read. I was not to do anything that would tire me. A kitten, my companion, slept on top of my bed covers or played with a string I pulled around.

Sometimes I was carried to the living room or another bedroom in our farm house. On hot summer days, I enjoyed lying on a hammock stretched between two trees on our front lawn. Fluffy white clouds moved across the sky, and I named the different shapes. I watched the kittens that were playing and chasing each other under the long back porch. Our big black dog, when not with my Father or two brothers, sat on the grass beside me. I would pet his head and talk to him.

Every afternoon I looked forward to my mother reading to me for an hour. I loved listening to stories from *The Children's Friend* magazine or a thick Bible story book that had both colored and black-and-white pictures.

I enjoyed the stories from the Old Testament: of Noah building the ark, the animals coming by themselves to be saved from the flood, and why we have rainbows; how Abraham's faith was tested; how Isaac got a good wife named Rebekah; how Joseph, who had dreams, was sold into Egypt, resisted temptation, became next in authority to the great Pharaoh and with wisdom given by God, saved many people, including his own family; of how baby Moses, who was saved from death because his mother put him in a basket on the great Nile river, would become an Egyptian prince and then lead the children of Israel out of Egypt and later bring to our world the Ten Commandments given him by Jehovah; of Joshua marching around the city Jericho until the walls fell down; the loyalty and love of Ruth for Naomi; of the boy Samuel hearing Jehovah's voice when he lived in the temple helping the high priest Eli; of Saul, the first king of Israel, so jealous of David who, with only his sling shot, had the courage to stand up to the giant, Goliath; of wise King Solomon, saving the baby for its true mother; of the prophet Elijah showing the 450 prophets of Baal who was the true God of Israel; of Jonah, who learned obedience when he was swallowed by a big fish and came out again; of Daniel who was protected when he was thrown into the lion's den for praying to the God of Israel; and of brave Queen Esther who saved her people. I didn't know this at the time, but these stories were teaching me the difference between right and wrong and were helping me want to do good things too.

I imagined hearing the angels singing to announce Jesus Christ's birth. I pictured how smart and courageous Jesus was to talk to the learned men in the temple when he was only twelve years old.

I was learning to love Jesus for all the good things he did: miracles of healing the sick and raising the dead and feeding thousands of people with only a little food. How wise but kind he was when people tried to trick and hurt him. I didn't understand then all about the Garden of Gethsemane or why he was nailed on a cross, but I realized that he loved his mother and the little children. He even calmed the winds and the waves.

Saul had a vision on the road to Damascus. When he understood who Jesus really was, he became the Apostle Paul, the greatest missionary. Paul walked and sailed to many different places to spread the gospel and help converts in the various churches. He was so educated and learned that he could talk to anyone and so courageous that he was not afraid of anything. He was one of my heroes because he changed when he was wrong.

Though both my tonsils had been taken out when I was six years old, a doctor found that a piece of one tonsil had grown back and was infected. He believed that if it was taken out, I would get well. But I must get strong enough to survive the operation.

I had the operation and soon began sitting up a little each day. I felt shy eating meals with my family at the kitchen table. I had to learn to walk again, but my legs gradually became strong. I practiced walking a little each day.

In early November 1940, my big brother Merrill carried me into the tabernacle where I was baptized. I had turned eight years old seven months before. My father who was recovering from an operation couldn't be there.

Through all these months, my special mother had many worries and concerns. I hope she knows how much I love her. Because of her reading to me, I came to love the Bible and our dear Savior, Jesus Christ.

In the spring of 1940, a way to isolate and purify penicillin from its mold was found. A new era for medicine began. The first test of penicillin on a human being came in 1941. There was little penicillin available, but soon daily miraculous cures were reported from all parts of the world. By 1945, the Florey-Chain research team had found a way to produce penicillin in large amounts. Prompt treatment with penicillin generally prevents rheumatic fever from developing. -- from The World Book Encyclopedia

THE HAMMOCK, A SWINGING COUCH

The summer I had to stay in bed, I was often taken outside to lie in the hammock to have fresh air. I loved lying under the big, leafy tree. I would look over at our little white stone house with the long, wide porch. I watched the kittens playing with each other, running in and out under the porch. If Old Ned, our big black dog, was not gone with my father or two older brothers, he would come and sit close to the hammock. He liked me to pet his head. He panted a lot, his long red tongue hanging out.

Lying in the hammock, I enjoyed watching the big, white fluffy clouds moving across the blue sky. It was a peaceful place to be – with the animals, the green lawn and trees, and the sound of honey bees in the flowers and bushes.

I still love to be out in the great outdoors. Heavenly Father made a beautiful world for us.

COD LIVER OIL

My mom took a nursing course before she married which made her health-conscious. I still can't say that I like orange juice because every time I had a sniffle or flu, which was often, she dosed me with castor oil along with fresh-squeezed orange juice. Ugh. But I'm still alive. When the Raleigh traveling salesman came to our house, she bought cod liver oil pills. They were candy coated, and I chewed up plenty of them. Mom had to keep the bottle away from me.

When I was the last kid at home, on some Saturday nights, my mom would tell me to beg my dad to take us to the picture show in the neighboring town. That meant he would have to stop his farm work sooner than usual to get the cows milked, eat supper, and get ready. The shows were usually double-feature murder mysteries and cowboy shows. Maybe that is why one of my favorite authors is Louis L'amour who is good at writing description – enough, but not too much. He is a great story-teller, in my opinion. I like learning the history of our country, and he is a master researcher. I also love watching *Bonanza* on the TV. Adam is real yummy, isn't he?

I feel like I grew up much like a weed, grabbing water and sunshine where I could. But I never tried to or wanted to squeeze out the flowers. That has never been part of my nature. A sister, six years older than I, was my closest sibling. Since my two big brothers and oldest sister were even further apart from me in years, I was left to create my own entertainment.

I've had an unusual life. I've tried to make the most of it and see the glass half full rather than see it half empty. I'm grateful that I, as well as my family, have been protected and blessed through all the challenges and experiences.

I CAN PLAY THE PIANO

My big brother Merrill was home from school with the flu. I was home too, recovering from my illness. I attended third grade at school only a few months in the spring, but I still passed the grade. I don't remember doing school work at home, but I must have done some to be able to pass. I've always liked school.

Merrill could play songs by ear if he knew the tune. He decided to teach me to play "My Wild Irish Rose."

First, I must be able to play the melody (tune) with my right hand, one note at a time. Next, I learned the C chord, the F chord, and the G chord with my left hand. Then it was time to put both hands together. By watching my brother, I quickly learned to do this. It was fun!

Later on, I learned to read music. I still enjoy making up my own left hand accompaniments to melodies that I play with my right hand. This is called improvising.

THE STOCKING CAP

When I was in an early grade in school, I think my mother was upset about something one day. She rolled my hair up tight against my head with a cold curling iron and then cut off my hair.

Even as a child, I was so ashamed of how I looked that I wouldn't take off my stocking cap in school for about three or four months. The other kids never pulled it off to tease me, and it finally it grew out again.

I thought of this incident one day many years later while I was being a substitute teacher at a high school. I noticed one boy wearing a stocking cap; the weather or temperature of the school room did not justify that.

I caught his eye and beckoned for him to come to my desk. I was trying to be discrete so as not to call the other students' attention to the fact that I wanted to talk to him. A folding chair was nearby. I indicated that I'd like him to sit down for us to talk quietly.

I smiled at him and in a pleasant tone of voice said, "I'm wondering why you are wearing that stocking cap on such a warm day. It reminded me of something that happened to me once." I paused, and I think my manner and his curiosity gave him the security to speak. He said, "I hate my hair cut. I don't want anyone to see it." I said, "I understand how you feel." Then I told him what had happened to me. I don't know how his situation played out, but he knew that I was a caring substitute teacher.

In grade school I loved swinging around a huge metal

pole we called "The Giant Strikes." Out of the top of the pole came long chains that held short metal bars we could hang on to while we lifted our legs off the ground and swung around the pole.

One time, in winter, I didn't keep my feet up high enough. I went dragging through a small lake of mushy snow and water and got wet to my waist. My long-legged underwear and long brown cotton socks were soaked.

It was too cold to send me home. Teachers didn't call home. The teacher had me sit close to the big pot-bellied stove in front of the room so I would dry out. The long brown stockings were hung close by. I had to sit for hours by the big hot stove to dry out my long-legged underwear. It was mortifying because now all the kids in the room knew I wore long underwear under my long brown stockings. None of the other girls did, though they did wear long brown stockings. But the kids were kind and didn't tease me. We never made fun of each other about anything. If tales were told of kids' misbehavior, parents took action.

I REMEMBER WHEN . . .

Most kids don't like studying history in school. What they don't know is that they are MAKING history. I made history too.

My first and second grade teacher at the little white rock school was Mrs. Lorena Smith. She was "nice," and what that term means to grade school children, only they can tell. Kids can make very decided judgments. To me "nice" meant not being afraid of her – I didn't care about or pay attention to what she wore – just feeling that her image and voice were comfortable.

She taught us to read using phonics. I loved the Dick and Jane books. Of course recess was the best, but I was often anxious about Jerry leading Kay, Keith, and Harold to gang up on me so he could kiss me. I seemed to be the only girl with this problem. If I was asking for it, I didn't know how. I didn't dare tell anyone.

When weather permitted, we all enjoyed the swings, flying around on The Giant Strikes, playing hop scotch, jump the rope and tag. In later grades, playing baseball was THE MOST fun.

During bad weather – in Idaho it could be FREEZING cold – we stayed in the school and played jacks and tick tack toe and hangman on the blackboard. As my best friend Charole and I approached puberty, we loved to practice dancing in the back of our room. Two steps forward and one step back. None of the other kids did. I think we just liked rhythm. She was the boy part and I was the girl part.

In the winter it wasn't much fun when "nature called". We dreaded having to go outside to the outhouse. In better weather, it was a good excuse to have a break from school. We were not forced to wait for recess and noon to relieve ourselves – a kindness. Because the outhouse had only two holes and we had to take care to avoid getting splinters from the boards we had to sit on, I doubt all the kids could have handled "the need" only at noon and recesses. We had one outhouse for boys and one for the girls at opposite ends of the school yard. Because of the stench, we didn't linger, but we did poke along going and coming. We would write our name on the blackboard before leaving, and most of us didn't abuse the privilege by taking too long or going too often.

We girls always wore dresses. The kids who had a long way to walk would wear long pants under their dresses, then take them off at school until time to walk home. In the early grades, many girls wore long brown cotton socks to keep warm in the winter. We also wore snow pants, boots, mittens and warm parka hats. Our hair and clothes were not a concern. There was no place to primp; there was only one tiny, cloudy mirror over the drinking fountain in the dark, cold hallway where our coats and boots were left. We students got along well, and I don't think school was a dreaded experience to anyone.

I LIKED MONDAYS

Many people think of Mondays as being "down" days. I liked Mondays. Mom would do the week's washing using the Maytag wringer washer and twin rinse tubs. Hot water was heated in the reservoir attached to the kitchen stove. When I was not in school, I helped hang all the clothes on the outside clothesline.

I loved our food: white beans and ham hocks, yummy rice pudding cooked in the oven, baked potatoes, and homemade whole wheat bread. And there was always fresh milk from our cows. Mondays were predictable, and I liked that.

Flatirons, kept on top of the kitchen stove, pushed to the back out of the way, were kept hot and ready for use. At night, in wintertime, we wrapped them in newspapers and put them under the covers at the foot of the bed. My dad liked to warm his backside by sitting on the open oven door that was supported by the old iron stool which had 101 uses.

The side porch on the big old rock house looked out on Mom's flower garden. Besides the weeds, there were peonies, a tall snowball bush, tiger lilies, purple and white lilac trees, bachelor buttons, phlox, and black-eyed Susans. There were also lots of petunias, pansies, and marigolds. I think we had the only Oriental poppy in the community. Mom kept African violets and geraniums in the house year 'round.

I liked this big old rock house, though it was spooky at

night because the front porch was covered with thick vines and the side porch was very dark. There were no neighbors nearby and no real locks on the doors. I remember when I was not more than fourteen, the folks went somewhere overnight – a funeral or something – and I was left home alone. A neighbor came and milked the cows night and morning. It was a traumatic experience because I kept thinking of the man through the field who went on periodic "benders" during which no one knew where he had been or what he had done. But I did live through it!

BEWARE OF ELECTRICITY

Farmers sometimes put up electric fences to keep the farm animals from going into fields where they should not be – like the alfalfa fields. If a cow ate the growing alfalfa, it could bloat and die. Beware! Any single wire could be an electric fence.

Nearly every week of the summer I visited the neighbors who lived across the road and down a ways. I played games outside with their three young children. The family subscribed to a newspaper that had a lot of funny papers as part of the Sunday paper. Loretta, the mother, would give me the funny papers to take home if I would gather them up from all over the house.

One time, during the irrigation season, the children and I were playing tag in the back yard. An electric wire was strung from the back porch out to the field. It was above the reach of the children, but because everybody had clothes lines strung up in their back yard, I must have thought the wire was a clothesline, or I wasn't thinking at all. I reached my arm up and grabbed it.

The yard was wet from recent irrigation, so it strongly conducted the electricity. The current shot through me. I screamed, and I was doing a lively dance trying to let go, but I couldn't. All I could do was change hands. The children stood gaping, wondering what had happened. Their mother ran out to learn the reason for the screams. Seeing the situation, she ran to the porch and threw the master switch. I dropped to the ground, and I had to be helped into the house to rest for a while. It was a close call.

I had a harmless encounter with electricity because of one of my older brothers. He was a whiz concerning electricity. He "wired" his car. A person could not sit on the back seat. My Dad sent him on an errand to a neighboring town. I begged to go with him for the ride. It was a ride alright. All the way there and back I could not sit down on the back seat because of the electrical shocks. By this time, though I was only thirteen or fourteen, I was five feet eight inches tall. Being hunched over all that time was very tiring. He had no mercy; he just laughed at me.

Because of my brother's experiments with electricity, we were not bothered at Halloween. He wired the front fence and gate. If a trick-or-treater touched any part of the fence, they'd get an electrical shock. At this time, Halloween definitely meant tricks. We were one family that didn't have any tricks done, such as our outhouse tipped over, our animals abused, or things carried off.

MY HEAVEN ON EARTH

I awake to the sound of milk buckets clanging and the slam of the hall door which opens onto the screened back porch. My dad goes into the cold bathroom to wash up. Then, opening the door into the kitchen, he is ready for the breakfast that my Mom, wearing house slippers and a big apron over her dress, is fixing at the wood/coal burning stove. As always, Dad is hungry as a bear.

In my upstairs bedroom, I slide out of bed, stand on the little throw rug on the cold linoleum floor, and look out my window that faces west. I hear a car coming, then catch a glimpse as it whizzes by on the two-lane, paved highway.

I see our neighbor across the road, shovel in hand, irrigating his field of potatoes. Many clumps of willows, not too far distant, hide the slow running water of a slough. I wonder about the people who live in the old farmhouse beyond.

The sun is shining in a blue sky with big, fluffy white clouds. I want to hurry and eat my breakfast, pester my mom about any chores she needs me to do and then be out in that wide, wonderful world. My cats, the kittens, and Tippy dog will welcome me to another new day.

The old white stone house on the farm and our eighty-acre ranch a few miles away will always be a part of me. Every April I get homesick for the farm.

INVITED GUEST

When I was about twelve years old, my big sister Beth invited me to spend a weekend at her Idaho Falls nursing home dormitory. She was now an instructor in nursing. What a great time it was for me. Saturday afternoon she took me to *The Song of Bernadette,* the popular black-and-white movie. I was in seventh heaven. On Sunday, I went to her Jr. Sunday School where she was the chorister.

Some Saturdays I went with my dad to Idaho Falls. He was a farmer, but he also spent some time selling life insurance. He and a partner had an office in Idaho Falls. When she could, Beth came home with us for the weekend.

On those Saturdays Dad would give me a quarter to buy a bag of candy at Woolworths. While he was busy, I would run the streets alone. I always walked to the nursing home by the hospital to see Beth. I never was afraid. I felt grown up and enjoyed the freedom. I think I had an extra amount of adventurousness.

SUMMER FUN

There was an irrigation canal across the highway from my best friend Charole's house. On days she wasn't pulling weeds on her parents' farm we went swimming in the canal. Sometimes other kids came to swim too. It was fun.

I didn't know how to swim. There were no swimming lessons to take and no one to teach me. I didn't want the other kids to outdo me, so I pushed my body out across the water, took turns splashing one arm and then the other arm, all the while kicking my legs up and down. It worked. I could swim.

Swimming a few times on a family or church outing at Heise Hot Springs or the longer drive in the opposite direction to Green Canyon Hot Springs was like a real holiday, especially when there would be a picnic too.

Every summer our church would have a big party at the sand dunes above St. Anthony. It was fun. There was always a watermelon bust too. All we wanted to eat. Yummy! Summer evenings in Idaho are the best.

RIDING MY BIKE

My dad helped me learn to ride our big boy's bike. I loved it. I spent lots of time riding the bike on the highway. I loved motion and still do. I took some spills, and my legs showed bruises. Girls didn't wear pants or Levis unless they were picking up potatoes or tromping hay during harvest times.

Sometimes a teenager from the Archer community south of us would come barreling down the highway and deliberately turn in to scare me. It did scare me! But he didn't stop me from riding the bike. The highway was the best place to ride. The Grover lane, close by, was only gravel and no fun to ride on. And it was easy to get thorns in the tires that caused a flat if I rode around the corral in back of our house. Whenever cars were coming on the highway, I always rode on the gravel shoulder to be out of the way. I've always been a daredevil, though I didn't think of myself as one. Maybe it's called being adventurous. Was I gaining experience for life situations that would require me to have lots of courage?

My friend Charole had a small Shetland pony she rode past my house and up the Archer Lane to take their cows to a pasture for the day. In the evening she had to bring them home again to be milked. Many times I rode my bike along with her. I would pester her to trade me. I loved riding Prince. She would give me a turn at least once.

If my bike had a flat tire, we both rode on Prince. When he got tired of us two big lubbers, he would buck. Whoever was on the front slid down to his ears. I was usually on the back and fell off. We laughed and climbed back on again. But we gave Prince some mercy too. Charole was very protective of her little sorrel-colored pony.

MY DOLL HOUSE

Our big white stone house had a long, vine-covered porch on the front and another porch on the north side without vines which looked out on my mother's flower garden. On the north porch there was an old lumpy couch. When anyone sat upon it, Daddy Longlegs spiders came out from their hidden nooks. I thought I was being brave to pick them up by one of their legs and shake them over the banister to the ground below.

On this side porch I made a doll house from two wooden orange crates that I stood up side by side. There were four rooms that needed some furniture.

We had a wood pile with various-sized chips of wood scattered about. I gathered them, cut pieces of colorful cloth, and sewed the cloth around the chips. Now I had furniture.

I had miniature dolls that lived in the doll house. I would play with them by the hour, making up their life events. I was being very creative. Nobody had suggested that I make the doll house or play with it as I did.

Sometimes as I sat cross-legged before the doll house, the Daddy Longlegs spiders would crawl over my legs. I just brushed them off. They didn't scare me.

MAKING A BIG PLAYHOUSE

My friend Joyce and her younger brother, Mack, sometimes walked down the road to play with me. There was an old wooden toilet lying on its side in the pasture next to our big white stone house.

We decided to make the toilet into a playhouse. We washed it thoroughly with rags and soapy water. We gathered flowers and stuck them in tin-can vases, and with pieces of cloth, we made curtains and nailed them up above the big wide window. With crayons we drew pictures on paper to hang around inside our house. It was fun, and we were proud of what we accomplished. We spent many hours making up and acting out our real-life plays.

On Sunday afternoons after dinner and before we had to get ready for church again in the evening, I sometimes walked up the road to Joyce's house to play with her and

Mack. Their mother always made homemade vanilla ice cream which I loved. I was sure to be given a large dish of this yummy treat.

THINGS I DID FOR FUN

Did I ever play with dolls? NO! I turned my cat, Jupiter, into a living doll. He ran every time he saw me. He didn't like me putting a doll dress and bonnet on him. I filled an empty Raleigh vanilla bottle with milk and put a lamb's nipple on it.

I put the squirming cat into my little green doll buggy, lying on his back bone, with rolled up doll blankets against both his sides to keep him in position. He seemed to sense that the bottle of milk was coming for he tolerated it long enough to suck out all the milk. Then, with one mighty kick of his back legs, the bottle flew out of the buggy, and he jumped out. It was a job for me to rescue the doll clothes he wore, but I did.

If the cows were a safe distance away, my dog Tippy and I played in the ditch over in the pasture. I liked trying to catch the water striders and polliwogs. I'd tell the big frogs to stop croaking at me; I wouldn't hurt their babies. It was trouble to hold up my dress so it wouldn't get wet. Tippy liked it when I threw sticks for him to retrieve. He kept up a joyful barking to tell me he was enjoying our fun.

When I felt restless, I climbed onto the roof of the barn and sheds and walked around, trying not to stumble or lose my balance and fall off. Also, I climbed on top of the chicken coop. It had a roof made of dirt clods, so I didn't walk around. It was fun finding a way to get up. I don't know if my mother knew I was doing these dangerous things. I wasn't about to tell her. In the middle of our field was a line of weird-shaped apple trees. I liked figuring out how to climb all of them. I didn't care about scratched up legs and arms. It was a miracle I didn't break my arms or legs. I never thought I might fall. I was having fun!

I AM AN ARCHITECT

Two huge poplar trees stood on our front lawn. My tire swing hung on a sturdy pole that stretched between them. Every fall many leaves fell off the trees. I enjoyed raking them into leaf houses. Lines of leaves divided the huge rectangular shape into a front room, kitchen, bedrooms, bathroom and porches. I also made other shape houses besides rectangles. It was fun being a creative architect.

I found furniture for my leaf houses. A bushel basket turned upside down became a table. Cinder blocks were couches. Beds were old pieces of blankets arranged on the grass. My imagination helped whatever I found become what I needed.

On windy days, it was frustrating when parts of the walls blew away. And Tippy, our dog, would run through the walls of my leaf houses to get attention. I think he liked it when I scolded him. His tail would wag. Then he would sit down and watch me rake the lines again.

MY HORSE

Because my friend Charole had a Shetland pony that I enjoyed riding sometimes, I really wanted to have a horse too. I even prayed to have a horse.

One day my father brought home a horse for me. It was part Shetland but as tall as a regular horse. The horse had been bought at an auction. Because it was tall, I felt some fear about riding it. My father put a bridle on the horse, helped me up on it, then led us around so the horse would get used to me. The horse acted all right a couple of times doing this, so my fear calmed down. I really was happy that now I had a horse.

On a Sunday afternoon my father was reading in our front room. I asked if he would put the bridle on my horse so I could ride it. I was riding the horse around the corral, so my father went back into the house.

Suddenly, the horse took off at breakneck speed, running through the corral, across the field, and up to the bridge over the big irrigation canal. I pulled hard on the reins to stop the horse, but it paid no attention to me. We reached the wooden plank bridge over the canal and suddenly it whirled around and started back to the corral. We were almost there when, suddenly, the horse bucked. I flew off, went sailing through the air, narrowly missing a tall hay feeder that I could have been impaled on. I lit hard on the ground. Though shaky, I got up unhurt and went bawling to the house.

My father came outside with me saying, "If you don't get back on the horse right now, it will know you are afraid, and you will never be able to conquer it."

I didn't want to get back on the horse, and I said so. But I wanted so much to have my own horse that I did get back on. It took all the courage I had.

The horse acted fine as I guided it around the corral. But my father was still out there watching, and he stayed until I wanted to stop riding.

Another day I rode the horse because my father stayed with me, but I was still afraid, and I said I didn't want the horse. My father took it to an auction, and that was that. All my prayers to have my own horse stopped.

HARVESTING THE HAY

The radio was bringing frightening news of World War II. Gas and sugar had to be rationed. My parents were worried about my brother Merrill, a sailor on a tanker in the Pacific Ocean. With Merrill in the Navy, I was needed to help with the farm work.

During hay harvest, I tromped the hay as my father and brother Hyrum pitched it up on the wagon. I kept my eyes open for mice caught in the piles of hay. My stomach felt weird watching Tippy jump on the nests of mice and swallow them as the hay was lifted from the ground. The mice ran every direction to escape, but the dog got most of them.

The team of horses waited patiently between times they were led to more piles of hay. When the wagon was loaded, we all rode to the corral. Now I straddled my legs across Old Ned's back and guided the horse to pull the cable which lifted the huge fork full of hay off the wagon and carried it to the haystack.

Old Ned stopped when I yelled "whoa" and pulled back on the reins. Then we waited while my father, on the haystack, pushed the big fork back and forth to position it just right. This was exciting to watch. If the fork was not positioned well, the hay could slide off to the ground, causing extra work and time.

When my father hollered, "Let 'er go" it was the signal for Hyrum, standing on the wagonload of hay, to jerk the rope connected to the fork. The fork would open and the hay dumped out on the stack.

Every summer on the Fourth of July, the hay harvest stopped, and we went into town for the parade, carnival and a picnic. To me, the carnival rides made it the best holiday of the year. I liked the excitement, but most of all, the movement.

SPECIAL REMEMBRANCES

After school, before practicing the piano, I liked to listen to a few radio programs. "House of Mystery" was my favorite.

I really liked October potato harvest. It was fun being out in the potato field with boys that were hired to pick the potatoes. I steered the truck or tractor down the potato rows to pick up the sacks of potatoes, then rode to the big spud cellar to dump the potatoes. "We'd better put an extra pile in the cellar for Lane," my father would say. I've always loved eating potatoes.

On Halloween I would go trick or treating. I walked the quarter of a mile to Charole's house, and together we went on down the highway, stopping at several houses. It was usually cold and windy before I reached home again. The vines on the front porch looked spooky in the moonlight. I was glad to get safely inside the house. I knew better, but I still worried that something lurking behind the vines might grab me.

On Thanksgiving Day it was fun playing Chinese Checkers and Rook. If the spud cellar had enough snow, I got the big long skies from the shed and skied down the cellar and out into the snow-covered field. Three or four times was enough; it was hard work carrying the skies back to the top of the cellar to go down each time.

Mr. Fowler, who taught the sixth, seventh, and eighth grades all in one room at our two-room white stone grade school was a favorite teacher. He was comfortable to be around and he often played baseball with us kids during recess and noon hours. He had no discipline problems; everyone felt that he was their friend. When the weather was too cold to play outside, he would ask me to play the piano and encourage the kids to gather around and sing songs. On Friday afternoons he gave everyone pictures of birds and flowers to paint with water colors. That was the start of my love of art. My best friend, Charole, and I often practiced our dancing – two steps forward and one step back, over and over again. One year, in fifth grade, she and I gave "plays" before both rooms. We dressed up, gossiped about several kids, and ate raw onions to shock everyone. They sat on my stomach for a week. It was creative but it was a wonder we were allowed to do this. I don't think our parents ever knew. Charole had sneaked the dresses, hats and purses.

    On a camping trip to Yellowstone Park, it was exciting to be stuck on top of Jackson Pass because our Ford passenger car had developed vapor lock. Through the tall, stately pine trees steam could be seen rising from the distant geysers and hot pots. When the car recovered, we carefully descended the hairpin turns to the bottom of the pass, safely crossing the high mountain range.

    We pitched our tent at the Old Faithful campground and then ate food my father cooked over a campfire. The Postum was yummy in the cold mornings. We watched Old Faithful go up and walked on the board walks to see the hot pots. The Morning Glory Pool was my favorite. In the evening we sat on bleachers and watched park rangers feed the bears. It was a trip never to be forgotten.

OUR FARM

    Our big white stone farmhouse was set back away from a two-lane paved highway. Two old tall poplar trees flanked the side of the lawn that was fenced off from the dirt driveway leading to the back yard. My rope swing, with a cut-out rubber tire to sit in, hung from a pole that spanned the two trees. I spent many hours pumping the swing up as high as I could go. What exhilaration! Or I would twist the swing up until my breath was almost choked off and then lift my legs and go into a dizzy whirl. When the swing was back to normal, I'd jump out and try to walk straight.

The kitchen windows of the house looked out on the back yard. A long tin shed sheltered the large and small Farmall tractors. Next to the shed was a tall wooden granary which held mounds of golden wheat, scurrying mice and rickety stairs leading to an attic loaded with cast-off junk. Sometimes I gingerly climbed the stairs, stepping carefully to avoid the gaping holes. I thought I was brave and daring to go up to the dark, gloomy place alone. I didn't stay long.

The chicken coop, made of logs with a dirt-clod roof, was next to the granary. Sometimes I had to gather the eggs. A few of the hens would not be shooed off their nests. I hated reaching under them to get their eggs. They would grab hold of my skin and twist. It hurt!

In the early evening when Mom opened the chicken coop door, the chickens swarmed out, thoroughly enjoying their freedom. Before we went to bed, someone shut and locked the coop door. The chickens had already gone to roost for the night.

Next to the chicken coop was the corral made of poles. In one corner was the smelly pig pen. Sometimes I carried out dishwater slop to pour in their trough. I wondered how they could roll around in such filth, grunting in obvious bliss. I couldn't get away soon enough.

The cows in the adjoining pasture would come to the corral when it was milking time. At times their obstinate, determined behavior left lots to be desired, and they were so unpredictable. I'm still afraid of cows! One time Old Bossy stepped on my foot. I screamed and yelled, but she wouldn't move. Dad jumped up from his milking stool, grabbed a pitchfork and poked her rump. Oh, blessed relief!

It is dusk. The countryside is quiet. Cows are bedded

down, chewing their cuds. Insects are hushed. Birds cheep sleepily. The kittens, curled together, are asleep, and their mothers are out roaming the fields for mice and gophers. Tippy, lying on the back porch, his muzzle on his front paws, opens one eye occasionally as he keeps watch.

These are a few things I recall about our farm in Idaho. Every April I feel homesick. Does that prove you can take the girl out of the farm, but you can't take the farm out of the girl?

I CAN DRIVE!

When I turned fourteen, I could get my driver's license. I would drive our little black coupe puddle-jumper which didn't have very good brakes. My dad was too busy to take it to town to get them fixed, and I didn't have sense enough to be scared to drive. It was war-time; people did what they had to do. Mom couldn't drive, so I'd take her to town, about nine miles away, to get a few groceries. She traded our milk that was picked up in front of the house for butter and cheese.

One time, when we were almost home from town, a car, coming fast toward me on the two lane highway, began to pass the load of hay that I was just coming to. There I was, in the way. Fortunately, the *steep* borrow pit on the side of the highway had no water in it, so I drove the passenger side of the car down into the borrow pit, while holding tight to keep my side of the car up on the shoulder of the highway. It was a wonder we didn't tip over, but that gave room for the car to get by. Then I drove the puddle-jumper back onto the highway, and we went on our way.

A similar incident happened in Illinois while I was driving my missionary companion's car to Nashville, Tennessee. Muriel marveled at how cool she thought I was.

I said, "I've done this same thing before." Both times, head-on collisions were averted. I know I have guardian angels.

But one time, I didn't appear to be a good driver to my dad. I was maneuvering the little Farmall A tractor to help him clean out a ditch on our farm. He was managing the hand plow the tractor was pulling. I was having a *hard* time holding the tractor from climbing the sides of the ditch. Dad got impatient and finally yelled, "I don't know how you can be so good in your music when you are so damn dumb on this tractor."

I did a lot of tractor driving all my teenage years – both the little Farmall A and the big Farmall H tractors. Also, I had a steady foot driving the big truck down the rows to pick up the sacked potatoes to haul to the cellar where they were stored, waiting for a good market price. The wrath of hell would have descended on me if I had allowed the truck to jerk and spill the sacks of potatoes on the field. It didn't!

TEENAGE TRIUMPH

I was scared. But I had the piece memorized. I could do it.

It was the first assembly of the school year. I was fourteen, a freshman at Madison High School in Idaho. The auditorium was jammed – about 400 kids and their teachers. My name was announced, and the announcer said I would play a piano solo, "Valse Arabesque."

I was sitting near the back of the auditorium with my friend, Charole. I hurriedly walked to the front of the auditorium and sat down at the grand piano.

My fingers flew over the keys – up and down, up and down. "Valse Arabesque" is a busy, breath-taking piece.

I finished and swiftly walked back up the aisle to my seat. All the time, the loud clapping threatened to raise the roof off the auditorium.

That was my debut as one of the best pianists of Madison High School.

AM I A SNEAK OR WHAT?

In high school I was one of those "hay seeds" from the farm who rode the bus nine miles to town each day. But my ability to play the piano so well was like a red carpet for me. I *loved* high school. Everyone knew me in our 400-student high school. I was friendly, and I gave all the students my smile with a friendly "Hi." I played for most of the assemblies we had every Friday, and accompanied the Mixed Chorus and Girls Glee. I spent a lot of noon hours eating my lunch on the piano bench in the auditorium to practice with kids for all the programs. I was voted president of the newly formed Glockenspiel Club. I was also historian of the Pepper Club. I felt real smart wearing our white sweater with colored emblems, my black skirt, saddle oxfords and anklets.

My dad let me quit wearing long-legged underwear when I went to high school, but he would not give permission to take off my *long* brown stockings. which were held up by elastic garters. He was paranoid because of my health history, and he always wanted to keep me bundled up like a hot house plant. At this time, in my family at least, kids were seen and not heard. To argue about what I wanted? Never heard of such a thing. Obedience was taken for granted.

All of us girls wore slacks under our dresses or skirts because there was no heat on the cold school bus. Then we took them off when we got into the school restroom. I sneaked the slacks AND my long brown cotton socks off at school and put on anklets until it was time to go home. Not even my mother knew. What kids won't do to be like their peers.

Another time I remember being a sneak was when I ate dirt. I don't remember being nagged to eat or being stuffed as a young child. I neither looked forward to eating nor dreaded meal times. One summer, I would run my finger around the car tire rims and then put it in my mouth. The fine silt tasted so good. I craved it. It tasted wonderful. I've read since then that there is potassium in dirt and that that particular mineral is essential to proper growth. It wasn't a time when people took vitamins and minerals. I must have been in a growth spurt and really needed it.

A FEW OF MY MOST EMBARRASSING MOMENTS

The summer I was sixteen I was asked to go to a show in a neighboring town with a guy who looked to me like Tyrone Power, the movie star. He was about seven years older than me. He was a cool, cool dude, home for the summer from a university in another state. It's a wonder my folks let me go; I hadn't gone on many dates before. I was both excited and scared. He drove me in his family's big green Cadillac-looking car; I don't remember what make it really was.

He bought our tickets, and we walked into the theater. It was dark. Coming in from outside, I couldn't see a thing. Because it was so dark, he led me to our seats, and he sat down first. I sat down, not realizing the seat had popped back up again and wasn't there. I grabbed the seat in front of me with both hands to keep from sitting on the floor. My long legs were going back and forth under the seat in front of me. I was chinning myself on the seat before me. My feet scuffled to get under me so I could stand up. The movie had started, so he probably did not hear that. Finally, I made it and then tried sitting down again. This time, I held the seat down with one hand as I sat down.

In the pitch black darkness he would have had to have unusually good eyesight to see such a hilarious shenanigan. But, because I was trying so hard to act grown up, I didn't reason well, and I felt totally mortified, thinking he probably had seen me. I could have cried.

Well, I survived that evening, and I must not have been too weird for company because he asked me to go play tennis another day. Me play tennis? What is that?

Well, I won't bore you about that afternoon. It was a circus you can believe. Well, there's a first time for anything. He was always telling me how cute I was.

P. S. His mother unexpectedly told me a few years later, "Elaine, you could have had him. He liked you. And I wanted you." I told her that my father had stomped his foot down, and I obeyed.

* * * *

When I was a senior in high school, I was invited to go on the junior college special outing by a fellow I had dated several times. I loved the beautiful corsages he would give me for the several formal dances at the college.

He drove all of us; two couples were in the back seat. We arrived at Yellowstone National Park, a few hours drive away, to see the sights. It was a beautiful spring day.

The steam from the hot pots we were walking around on the board walks to see straightened my hair. All the curl vanished. My hair became as lanky as my legs. This was not the style at the time. I tied on a skimpy scarf which didn't make me feel any better, but I hoped it hid a little bit of my straight straw stack.

I did my best to be good company anyway, but it was

a long day. I should have just laughed and joked about it, but my self-esteem wasn't that secure. Also, I was the youngest of the group and not a college student. Emotions. Aren't they crazy sometimes? No one commented about my hair. My date, a perfect gentleman, remained his pleasant, comfortable self. I still love Yellowstone Park.

* * * *

My first blind date was an arranged affair. I didn't know if I wanted to go; normal dates made me anxious. But I thought I'd better be a good sport. Dean turned out to be nice looking and very nice, but quiet. He was also some years older than me. I felt self-conscious, stupid, and inexperienced about initiating small talk. I think Dean was shy too. It was a quiet date. I decided I hated blind dates, and I have tried to avoid them ever since.

For years, people have been trying to get me married a second time. They might as well give up. I like this poem that I did not write. It is on a little plaque I bought.

> To live your life in your own way
> To reach for the goals
> you have set for yourself
> To be the you that you want to be
> That is success.

I could tell more incidents, but I won't. Growing up – if one ever really does grow up, I'm not sure I have – just isn't easy.

JOBS, JOBS, AND MORE JOBS

Besides my job as tractor driver for several summers on our farms and helping my mother, I gave private piano lessons. I would drive to neighboring communities and teach students in their homes. The summer I was twenty-one, I cleaned cabins in Moran, Wyoming while waiting for my husband to finish his basic training in the Army. He was stationed in Denver, Colorado. There, I knocked on doors to get piano students, sold *Childcraft* so I could have a set of my own, and sold *Avon* cosmetics.

My sister, her husband and her young child visited us for a couple of days. She suggested that with my one year of typing in high school, I might get some temporary secretarial jobs. I did, and it was great! My first job was with Lion Oil Company in downtown Denver. Wow! Was this little farm girl grown up to ride city buses to work every morning in such a huge city.

The foxy head secretary had me decipher and type up on the typewriter the collected scribblings of the oil scouts as they had sat on an oil well. I about drove her crazy. I was determined to do a good job, but she couldn't read some of them either. My best help came from one of the scouts who came in the office at times. He felt sorry for me. He'd show me pictures of his wife and two cute kids as he tried to help me with the worst ones. I loved that guy!

One day, it was Secretary's Day in the city. We all walked to the other Lion Oil building, and in a huge room with a big circular table, we had a delicious lunch. The dapper boss, one of the bosses from my office, stood up and proposed a toast to everyone with their martinis that were already poured for each person. He called out my name to stand and toast with him – the only one. It shocked me. I went beet red and sat there shaking my head, "No." It is against my religion to consume such drinks; I would have no part in it. I was dressed like a hayseed compared to the other females. I wished I could disappear. I think he wasn't much admired by everyone for doing that.

After finally finishing my work at Lion Oil Company, I worked a few months for Investment Securities. There I answered the phone and took messages. The boss's wife, his secretary, was home in bed trying to hold on to their baby. Next, I worked for World Insurance in their home. I did secretarial odd jobs. I appreciated all of these jobs. They were a great experience. I have always loved learning new things.

Later on, back in Utah, I gave piano lessons, worked briefly for a real estate company and then a picture framing company. I taught a few classes at a behavioral boy's school while getting my teacher's certificate. Then I moved to Wyoming for my first full-time teaching job. Oh, yes, I had sold New York Life insurance until I realized I was neglecting my children and quit.

I was a top seller for McKinley Institute, selling business and real estate packs over the telephone to call-ins from all over the United States until McKinley moved out of town. I sold Perma Pack foods. I always had piano students. Life has never been boring.

THE PROFESSIONAL MUSIC WORLD

Being a piano accompanist has helped me gain special knowledge about the artistic production of music. I feel I have been a better piano teacher because of those experiences. I accompanied the vocal lessons for artist-teacher Nina Kochetz, who was living in Los Angeles. She had been a prima donna in Russia. Her accompanist for concerts and recitals had been the famous pianist, Rachmaninoff.

Though Nina Kochetz had retired from the concert stage, her daughter was a professional singer in Los Angeles, and she wanted to hire me to be her regular accompanist for recitals and concerts. She was complimentary about my ability to sight read and to follow her. I would have been well paid.

At the time, we were living, only temporarily, in South Pasadena. With two very young children and the need to drive the freeways a lot, it was not feasible for me to be her accompanist, though I would have loved to be. She was disappointed when I explained why I could not.

I have also accompanied lessons for Ingenuus Bentzar of Salt Lake City, a former Danish opera star, and Ray Arbizu who concertized several years in Europe. Both were retired from professional singing and teaching. I also played for other university vocal teachers.

I have enjoyed giving much time to sharing my music for community projects, in the churches, and with many individuals.

BEST NEIGHBOR

I was managing a dozen apartments, had 30 piano students in the afternoons, and three little girls, all under five years of age. One morning, after changing the year-old baby, I put her in the play pen in the corner of the living room by the front window. I noticed an older neighbor on her porch frantically waving her arms, beckoning for someone to come. Her house was across a very busy street. Nearby neighbors did not spend time in their front yards because of the traffic noise. They would not see her.

I stepped out on the porch and above the din of traffic yelled across to her, "Do you need help?" She had a towel pressed to her face, and she kept beckoning. I yelled, "I'll be right there."

My two little girls were behind me wondering why I was yelling. I turned and said, "Mommy has to go help Sister Scott. You both stay here, and don't follow me across the busy street. The baby is in the playpen, and she will be safe. I will come back as soon as I can. Be sure you stay here." They were obedient little ones, and I felt they would be all right long enough for me to go see what was Sister Scott's problem.

My neighbor saw me come out on the porch and start down the stairs. This gave her confidence that I was coming over, and she went into her house. I dodged the busy traffic safely, arrived at her house, and burst in the door. She was lying on the couch with a towel pressed to her face. She told me her husband was gone with their married son to their dry farm, and there was no way to reach them.

Because she was alone, she had panicked when her nose began to bleed. I fixed cold cloths for her face and then tried to call her daughter-in-law, but there was no answer. The bleeding stopped. I could see her fear of me leaving her, though she realized my three small children were alone. I told her I must go check on them, but I promised I would come back. This seemed to calm her, and I left.

I went back and forth four or five times and continued trying to reach her daughter-in-law. She never came. When Mrs. Scott seemed less anxious, I stayed home with my children. Her husband came home in a few hours.

Later on, my husband said that Sister Scott was telling neighbors and friends that I was "the best neighbor she had ever had."

Another time, one morning when my children were gone to school and I was washing the breakfast dishes and beginning food preparations for our evening meal, the telephone rang. It was a neighbor. "Elaine, I think I am having a heart attack. Can you come help me call for an ambulance and call my son? I have the phone numbers here."

I assured her I would be there immediately. I ran across the lawn and down a short incline to her house. I made the calls and then asked if she would like me to pray while we waited. This helped to calm her. Her son said he would meet her at the hospital, so after I saw her safely into the ambulance, I went back home.

Her appreciation was later evident in a sweet note she wrote about how my fast response and prayers had calmed her and had given her faith. Later on, I received a gift of a beautiful dark green Christmas wreath she had crocheted from yarn. It was decorated with small figures playing musical instruments. It has been a cherished gift, displayed on my front door for many Christmas seasons.

Our example Jesus Christ has said, "Love one another."

AN ANSWER FROM HEAVEN

I was in the early months of my last pregnancy. Though I was under a doctor's care, was trying to eat intelligently and was taking prenatal vitamins and minerals, I had no energy. One morning, after my husband had left for the day and our three girls were gone to their grade school, only little Danny and I were at home.

I stood at the sink, washing the breakfast dishes. Looking out the window I saw the many unsprayed yellow dandelions growing all over our yard. The thought came into my mind to make a dandelion herb tea to drink.

I dug up the dandelions, washed them clean with the backyard hose and then put them, roots and all, in a big stainless steel kettle and covered them with water. When the water came to a boil, I turned off the stove burner and let them sit.

After a few hours, I drained the dark dandelion water through a sieve into large glass bottles. I put the herb tea in the refrigerator and drank a cupful three or four times a day, with no sweetening. I made more batches of dandelion tea and drank it every day for a few weeks. It was a "lost and found" situation; our lawn lost all the dandelions, and I found more energy. Before this occurred, I did not know the full value of dandelion tea. I remember that my mother believed in natural things, but I think I had learned how to make an herb tea from a dear Naturopath and his wife.

> DANDELION ROOT (Taraxicum officinal). One of the best blood purifiers available. Rich in organic sodium; very good for anemia caused by a deficiency of nutritive salts. Effective as a liver cleanser. A very good, proven diuretic. Works well for the treatment of skin diseases, scurvy, and eczema. Also effective for fatigue, age spots, cramps, constipation, diabetes, hypoglycemia, jaundice, gall bladder and helps endurance.
> <u>Your Family Herb Guide</u> © 1982
> by author Austin John Bayberry

"For the earth which drinketh in the rain that cometh oft upon it, and bringeth forth herbs meet for them by whom it is dressed, receiveth blessing from God . . . " (The Bible: Hebrews 6:7)

RAISING CHILDREN

As soon as I brought my babies home from the hospital, they heard classical music. I loved music and wanted all of them to love it too. At that time it was not known that listening to music by the masters (Mozart, Bach, Beethoven, Schubert, etc.) helps a baby's brain develop faster and better.

For years I and the children went on regular trips to the public library and brought home *many* books. This was not being promoted by experts either, but I loved books and loved reading to them, especially from our ten-volume Bible Story collection that had beautiful pictures.

I made a chart that helped us get household chores done, gave us a way to work together and provided a way the girls could earn allowance money for birthdays, etc. I paid them to practice their piano lessons. I was their piano teacher. I did not pay for time practiced. I paid per page (not piece) of what was learned to my satisfaction and passed off. I had no trouble getting their practicing done or any resistance about who their teacher was.

One of my university piano students, who was majoring in Family Living, came to my home for a make-up lesson. She was curious about the chart, and I explained it to her – how jobs were assigned and paid for, etc. She said, "I'll have to tell my teacher about this chart." I told her we went on walks in the mountain behind us. We popped our own popcorn and smuggled it into the university's Varsity Theater on Saturday afternoons after stopping to buy candy. Tickets were cheap because I was on the piano staff. This was the kids' treat for getting their work done. Saturday evenings we watched the Lawrence Welk show with more treats. We often made no-bake carob oatmeal cookies that we all loved.

I paid for my son to have trumpet lessons from a university student. I thought it important for him to have a young man teacher. He loved the trumpet and his record player. The four girls had instrumental or ballet lessons besides piano lessons from me. We gave music programs as a family to the Blind Association and at the State Hospital chapel. They sang and played together. We were always very much appreciated.

I was telling all these things to the woman in charge of the Children's Justice Center when I rode with her to a seminar in Salt Lake City. My fee and luncheon were paid for because I was an advocate. She said, "Oh, how I wish the women we try to help would try half as hard to raise their families and had the desire to make a good home as you did. You are unusual."

I answered, "I wanted all my children, and I wanted them to know the important things are faith, music, good books, service, and work. They help build good self-esteem." She continued, "The women look around for someone else to do for them what they could do on their own."

We all like good strokes, and it was fun for me to share with her. I surprised myself, because I'm a private person.

FOOD, FOOD, FOOD

All through school, my five children did not go to school unless they ate a good breakfast first. I had my own stone grinder, and my pancakes were the epitome of creativity. My homemade cereals were also. I don't think I ever measured anything. I threw in several kinds of whole grains. Sometimes they were ground fine, and sometimes they were gritty. The pancakes turned out to be hefty, filling, and nourishing! I made the syrup. I knew they needed plenty of energy to go to school, do homework, their assigned chores, and practice the piano, flute, clarinet, and trumpet with no complaints of being tired.

I made several loaves of homemade whole-wheat bread every week. A slice of bread with jam was a standard snack after school. I made millet casseroles, rice-cabbage casseroles, hamburger casseroles, chili, tacos, hamburgers, potatoes, etc. And a salad was mandatory at every main meal!

Custard with cornbread was a treat. Cornflakes and grapenuts were also treats at times. We ate popcorn and no-bake carob-oatmeal cookies while watching Lawrence Welk on the TV every Saturday night. I made cakes only for Sundays: spice cake with delicious caramel frosting, chocolate cake, and plain cake with boiled white sugar frosting. We also had puddings and Jell-O. I seldom made pies. Oh yes, we baked cookies too.

The seed milk I learned to make the year we lived in Arizona helped keep us out of the doctors' offices. Someone once said, "Food is your best medicine." I believe that if it's the right kind of food. Baby Danny's crossed eye was straightened with a few ounces of fresh-juiced carrot juice a day. When my Champion Juicer finally wore out, I lost a best friend.

One time I was being teased by some family members about my food. Suddenly, five year old grandson Shay piped up, "I like your food, Grandma." He remembered times he'd stayed overnight with me and what we ate. "Out of the mouths of babes . . . " What's the rest of that saying?

CATHOLIC CHURCH ORGANIST

For a few years before I moved to Wyoming for my first public school job, I was the organist for Saturday night Mass at the local Catholic church. The older Father was very kind to me. I was paid $10.00 a week which helped our money situation.

For the midnight Mass on Christmas Eve, I also sang a vocal solo, *Gesu Bambino,* with two teenage daughters assisting me. Meladee accompanied me on the piano and Christine played a flute obligato. Though the church was full, and people were standing in the aisles, it was so reverent you could hear a pin drop. The Father gave a special sermon for the occasion. We felt it a privilege to provide the music for such a beautiful service.

One Saturday evening I had a bad scare. I always went nearly an hour early to practice the organ to be well prepared for the coming service. I walked in from the sidewalk and decided I would first go to the restroom which was in the basement. As usual, no one was around. Just before the service, the monks were always in their quarters attached to the back of the church; it was their dinner hour.

As I was walking into the ladies room, I heard footsteps behind me. I whirled around and saw a man was following me. He was not very well dressed, and he needed a shave. My fright must have showed on my face. He said, "Don't be afraid. I'm just hungry. Do you have a little money you could give me?" I had a couple of dollars in change which I gave him. Then he turned and left. Never again did I take that kind of a chance. I was protected, as I have been many times in my life.

A FEW EARLY SCHOOL TEACHING EXPERIENCES

While getting my teaching certificate at the university, I taught part-time at a behavioral boys' school. These were problem boys, ages 12-18 that had come from all over the nation.

The two English classes I turned into creating writing classes. A doctoral candidate from the University came to observe. She couldn't believe the creative stories and poems I had hung all over the bulletin board. She raved about it to the owner of the school. I think that the boys felt comfortable with me, and that let their imaginations and emotions come out.

One time, I gathered the boys in a circle (about a dozen), and I asked them to tell me how they felt about questions I would ask. Then we discussed their answers. When we finished, one boy said, "This has helped me more than the counselors do."

I also taught one music class. I could see that the boys

with their instruments could make up a little rock band. The owner couldn't believe his ears when he heard them play a few numbers on our little program. I couldn't either. I had turned them loose on their instruments and said, "When you come up with something, let me hear it." I was winging it, for I didn't know much about all those instruments.

First thing every morning, I taught a music appreciation class in the "dungeon". These were boys that are locked up twenty-four hours a day when they first come to the school until they get cleaned of their drugs and learn to accept discipline – about 20-25 boys, mostly older teens. I was locked in with them while a counselor observed us through a peep hole to see that they didn't hurt me. One time, a boy asked me, "Why aren't you afraid of us?" I answered, "Should I be?" He said, "Well, Betsy is." I never answered him.

In the "dungeon," there was only one black boy. He was tall and about 17 or 18 years old, a nice-looking boy. One morning, he kept interrupting my lesson by noisily blowing his nose. I knew the kids were waiting to see what I would do. Finally, I reached into my purse, pulled out a handkerchief and took a couple minutes blowing my nose. When I finally put the handkerchief back in my purse and lifted my head, the entire class burst out laughing. They roared with laughter. When they stopped, I went right on with my lesson as though nothing had happened, saying nothing about it. From then on, this particular boy was my slave. When he got out of the dungeon to take classes upstairs, every time he saw me he would in a most mannerly way ask me if he could get anything for me – a drink of water, some pop, or an apple.

I have tears as I write these experiences of touching the lives of young people.

WRITING POEMS

While I was living in Wyoming during my first public school job, my daughter Julie, a senior in high school, wanted my help with an assignment to write a poem or story about our move to Cowley.

We did, and that started me on a binge of writing many poems. They seemed to pour out of me. I think they were therapy for feelings and emotions. I'd like to get some of them published.

Moving To Cowley
By Julie and Elaine Watts, Nov. 1976
(Population of the town: 350)

When I first drove into Cowley
  I wished I was driving out.
  I thought we had gone back in time
    to Grandma's day.

We were welcomed by hordes
  of mosquitoes, eager to initiate us
    to the joys of country life.

The skies were pure and blue
  And mountains gave a feeling
    of protection and beauty.

The quiet of the still summer air
  was broken by the rumble
    of diesel trucks barreling
      down Main Street.

Most impressive were the well-kept
    grounds and unusual-type
        structure of the church.

Looking at the high school
    and the log building beside it,
        I thought,
    "I really have gone back
        to Grandma's day."

Then, noticing the grade school
    so modern, I thought "How can this be?"
Without settling that question,
    my attention turned next
to the boys practicing football
    on the field.

Dogs, dogs, and more dogs
    Surely there must be cowboys
    and horses too.

To my dismay, there was not
    even a show house in town.
        What could a teenager do?

Empty lots and weeds galore,
    Run-down buildings
        "Is that a store?"

Yummy-looking gardens brought
    food and friends.
        Showing us without a doubt,
            that we were welcomed
                and would be cared about.

Cowley Elementary Band
by Elaine Watts 1976-77

French horns, trombones, clarinets and flutes,
    A sax, also trumpets, sometimes using mutes.

Drums, snares, a timpani too,
    Elementary Band is strong – even with few.

A lady conductor, determined to do
    "You must keep the rhythm!"
    "Get each note right too!"

A baton which pounds to stop the din,
    "Why don't you watch? Go back again."

Her energy brimming, confidence too
    No time for fear; she pushes you through.

We're just normal kids, but she hasn't found out.
    Don't disappoint her.
We can be SPECIAL like she talks about.

WYOMING
by Elaine Watts Dec. 1976

Wyoming
    Vast stretches of land
I'm going there to lead the band.

Cowley, Lovell
    The destination
Nestled in the Bighorn Basin

Nature
    Lake among red hills
Water, a miniature Grand Canyon fills

Mountains
    Bighorn and Pryor
Picnics with wieners and fire

Isolation
    What do people do?
Read books, watch TV, write poetry too.

Exercise
    Bicycling, a good sport
Or go play at the tennis court

Talents
    Art and singing,
Good fellowship, enjoyment bringing

Farms
    Sugar beets and cattle
Trucks and tractors that rattle

Weather
    Dry, clear and cold
Autumn colors just like gold

Church
    The gathering place
To help many tomorrows face.

School
    Small classes,
Personal attention for the masses.

Children
    Eager and sweet
To watch succeed, a real treat

INVITED OUT
by Elaine Watts Dec. 1976

That fisherman with his wife in hand
    cutting holes in the ice
    hoping to entice suspecting fish

They would drop their line.
    Everything went fine.

Next, home they go
    over ice and snow
        with smell and taste in sight

To cook a feast
    share music last but not least
        and stories of long ago.

The accordion and organ kept busy with songs.
    A mouth organ, too, came into view,
    a duet with organ and song.

Improvising is an art.
    Some lost chords never start.
        But come time to part,
            we left glowing
        with warmth in our hearts.

(In memory of being invited to a delicious fish supper at the home of Mr. & Mrs. Jim Smith)

SOME OF OUR PETS

    Can you reflect back to simple things? Can you pause, look, feel, care and remember? There is more to experiences with God's creatures than meets the eye. Great men have always stressed the value of wonder. Creation is all around you.

I experienced much anguish when Tisha, my beloved companion for eight years, needed to be put to sleep. She comforted me through a serious illness one year. If I was lying on my bed during the day, she would jump up to be with me. At night, she never did that, somehow knowing that I needed undisturbed sleep. She was so intelligent, so good – human in many ways. My youngest daughter, Gloria, while living in England, had raised and lovingly disciplined her from the time she was a little kitten – about four years. When Gloria and her husband moved to the States, their apartment would not allow pets. I was happy to inherit her.

As a young teen, Gloria brought home a mistreated, half-grown stray kitten from a church meeting. "Yes, we can keep her." We named her Peggy. There were others: Dusty, Jupiter, Chocolate. Chocolate would "talk" to me. I was sleeping in one rare morning. He became concerned about me. Suddenly, I was startled awake by a very loud yowl.

Callie came to us as a stray cat with a chopped-off tail. Young son Dan was so excited when she finally decided it was safe – from under the kitchen table – to take some offered food. "Give her time to get used to us," I said. This beautiful, half-grown calico cat came to love and trust us. I don't recall all our pets, but we loved and cared for them, and that opened and stretched our hearts. Children, as well as adults, can be taught to be kind and to nurture.

As a youngster on the farm, I named Petunia for my mother's flowers. We called her Tuni. She birthed several litters of kittens. She was a wonderful mouser. I named one of her kittens Rosie. She was like her mother, only white with large black spots instead of all gray. Then there were Billie Whiskers, Midnight, and Tippie Dog, my pal and Old

Ned, the horse, who patiently took me up and down the canal bank many times. When I "graduate" from this life, I'm sure that many from the animal kingdom will welcome me. I look forward to that. I am comforted to know that they are in Heaven praising God.

FUN TIMES WITH CHILDREN AND GRANDCHILDREN

When I visited my youngest grandchildren after they moved to Idaho, we played a lot of hide-and-seek in their house. And we took excursions to the back of the nearby grade school to play on the playground equipment. The first time I went, they lived in a house in the middle of a large field with no near neighbors. Cody, about five years old, was so glad to see me that he couldn't stop telling me about everything. I loved it. We practiced making baskets into the hoop on the driveway. He and his younger brother, Brandon, had missed coming to be tended at my condo in Utah, with the near-by park and my cat Tisha that would hide, while Gloria went to her chorale practices.

One time when I visited, Cody was in school. Five-year old Brandon and I played the game, Uno. He could beat Grandma Music! We played it a lot that visit. When I was outside packing my car to leave, Gloria told me that he had come to her and said, "I'm already missing her." Gloria asked him, "Well, did you tell her?" He said, "No." She said, "Well, go tell her." He came outside and told me that. You can picture my response.

I've made a habit of gathering games, puzzles, books, toys, etc. at thrift stores so as to take a good-sized box full of surprises when I visit in Idaho. One time, Brandon said in response to all the things had I brought, "You are a *great* Grandma." That is how I first became a great grandma.

Another reason they looked forward to Grandma coming for a visit was that I treated them to a swim at the warm springs up in the foothills.

When Jed and Heather came along, my joy was doubled. We had lots of fun times. In 2010, for my Christmas card, first grader, Heather, drew a picture of her and me (stick figures) standing on the stairs leading up to my condo. She had printed, "To Grandma Mussick from Heather Dawn Muhlestein. I love you Grandma I defanatlee love you." Her mother told me it was her idea, and she did it without help.

An Education Week class I attended, *Children's Literature*, suggested writing and sending little notes to children and grandchildren. Since my five children and older grandchildren were grown up, I wrote and sent these mini poems to my three Idaho grandsons:

>Brandon's pictures are neat.
>He also can draw hands and feet.
>The landscapes are vivid,
>there's a rabbit named Pete,
>and his letters to Grandma are a treat.

>Cody drives the 4-wheeler.
>He swims and bike rides
>and from Grandma he hides.
>(Playing hide and seek.)
>In Scouts he will soar when he's an Eagle.

>Jed, his hair is bright red.
>He likes stories and tickles.
>And now he can climb out of bed.

I've cherished all the loving notes, pictures and poems given me through the years by all my children and the grandchildren.

There were times I took family and grandchildren to the *Mountain Spa* in Midway, a drive past beautiful lakes, and through mountains, about forty-five minutes away. After the swim I bought burgers and shakes or we ate the picnic we'd brought on a church lawn.

When my five children were young, I drove them up to Heber City to our dentist every summer. We had very few cavities. They were so excited to have this outing. We would go to the *Mountain Spa* afterwards. I didn't try to bottle-up their joy. I was happy too. The dentist, not appreciating their exuberance, demanded they play across the street on the grass and come in only one at a time for their exam.

We had fun taking many hikes in the foothills behind our house, sledding in the winter, and taking our own popcorn and candy to the university's Saturday-afternoon movies. My pass bought us tickets for a minimum fee because I was on the piano staff. These are all fond memories.

One time, my friends, Keith and Joyce Beebe from Mesa, Arizona, were visiting me. They brought the wife of his buddy from where they were staying by Great Salt Lake. Julie let my two young granddaughters go with us up the canyon to Sundance. We all hiked to Stewart Falls. There was never a complaint from the girls. After I took them home from our big day, which about killed off my company, Keith said about my special grandchildren, "I can't believe how good those little girls were." I had fun driving everyone to see the sights. It was a very special day for me.

I'll stop now with this original poem that my young

granddaughter, Anisha, had given me for my birthday. She drew and painted a picture illustrating it. It hangs on my wall.

    Dear Grandma
On this day
    When spring is out, and insects play
    Easter has come, your birthday too.

    Jesus is special, and so are you!

At night the colors of the sky
    run away

Leaving the sunset's
    Beautiful Bouquet.
        - Anisha

Angalee and Mike and Anisha and Brad have given me my first great-grandchildren.

POEMS FROM MY HEART

    Lonely Saguaro
You stand with upward reach
    To skies of azure blue.
An image fills my mind of one
Who hung with wounds and prickly thorns.

If I should touch your thorns and holes
Then could I understand His woes?
You help me think of Him above
Your arms encircling like His love.
    Oh Lonely Saguaro

Autumn Leaves
drift away
one
by
one
leaving emptiness
behind;
In time
replaced
by new
but never
the same.

Time
is fleeting,
yet everlasting
as
yesterday.

We realize
experiences
which touch
our lives
we
feel
today
will
be gone,
replaced
by time
yet
linger on.

Idaho Farm
Sometimes I wish
That time could turn back
To that Idaho farm I knew.

I'd wade in the ditch.
My dog would chase sticks.
He'd splash beside me again.

We'd walk in the field,
Hear a meadowlark's trill
Like silvery sounds of a flute,

See fluffy white clouds
High up in the sky
Watch ducks go flying by.

Though time moves on,
Memories are strong
Like wind on hot summer days.

Intangible, free;
No one can see, but I feel
They are part of me.

How Deep Is Our Faith In God?
When events taking place in our lives
Sometimes cause us to question the Plan
Of freedom to choose our own way
Still we know that our understanding
Lacks wisdom and often true sight.
He knows the end and beginning
And has promised all things work together
For good, if we trust in His love.

Time
Reflections upon time
    Yours and mine.
Where have we been?
What have we become?
    How will our lives
Be seen when done?
Will we meet that Being
    Bright as the Sun
And hear Him say, "Well done."

Journey
Swirling dust
clouded the desolate valley below.
    Distant cliffs,
misshapen and half hidden,
    were ominous.

    Apprehensive,
        I took in the scene
           while maneuvering my car
              upon the mountain highway.

My thoughts projected ahead,
moving me along the ribbon-like road
    into the thickening maze.
    I was alone, exposed
        to forces I could not define.

    Should I turn back,
content with familiar circumstances
    or brave the unknown,
conquering to gain new experiences?

I deliberated,
and through heightened awareness
touched back in time.
    This had happened before
    When leaving another sphere.

There, given my choice
I understood the journey could be lonely
    But I had made my way.
Courage would bring me through again.

The Calling Of A Mother
The sun goes down. I look without.
My thoughts reflect as those last rays
Mirror my needs, desires and hopes,
The challenges of this day and age.

I lift my eyes and search for strength
To lead, be steadfast for their need.
Each one a special soul
I know fulfillment as I live my role.

My Prayer
God help me be a shining light
Through shadow or storm, to keep in sight
A brighter day than I can see
With eyes veiled by mortality.

God help me be a pure delight
A scented flower with color bright
To give and share with seeming grace
A depth of beauty in heart and face.

The Ocean

The ocean with its waves
    lapping on the shore
Cool depths changing colors
    White seagulls soar.

Vast and endless reaching out
    Mystery and romance lure.
Cloudless skies burning hot
    The horizon shows no more.

Ships sail forth with trust
    A will to conquer – they must.
Like lives, deep and timeless,
    Many depths go unexplored.
The compass often not on course
    Heading to the other shore.

Longing For You

Longing for you

    Remembering
        the time
            we met
    in Spring

Our love
    was new
        like dew
    on flowering heather

    Rich
        with fragrance
            a purple hue.

COMMUNITY SERVICE

I became an advocate for an abused child in my community. After completing about 22 hours of training from therapists, nurses, police officers, etc., I was to take nine-year old Stephanie for a few hours one afternoon each week for an outing in the city. We both enjoyed going to the places we visited.

Also, I was a helper to a little girl from South America while she stayed with a family in the community to have physical therapy before returning to her home. The doctor, who made periodic trips out of the country to volunteer his service, brought her back to stay at his home to receive more of his help.

Maria was about ten years old. She and I couldn't talk to each other; we only gestured and smiled. She loved being taken to the Doll Factory and the Bean Museum, two places I remember.

For Christmas I gave both Maria and Stephanie beautiful medium-sized dolls, with lots of real hair, that I had bought on a sale. They loved the dolls. I was told that Maria never let go of hers and she even slept with it. Before she left for South America again, I cleaned out my jewelry box and gave her some bracelets and necklaces.

Two precious little girls, they touched my heart for good.

A TREASURED COMPLIMENT

I was playing the postlude on the organ for the church service. When finished, I turned around on the organ bench to get ready to leave. The young father of three children, ages five, seven, and nine that I teach all together in a group vocal, general music class in my condo living room, was waiting to talk to me. He had another very young child asleep on his shoulder.

He abruptly said, "I don't care if my children don't learn to sing." I looked at him, not sure I had heard him correctly. He said again, "I don't care if my children don't learn to sing." I could tell he had something else he wanted to say. I said, "You don't, why not?"

He answered, "I want them just to be around you. I like what you say and how you say it. I want them to have your influence."

Then he asked if I would give him the list of scriptures I had used in the talk I had given in the church service. I said I would. I could tell he still had something more he wanted to say. I smiled and looked expectantly at him.

He said, "Would you give me some vocal lessons? I'm awfully shy, but I'd like to sing better with my guitar."

In talking about his children, this man gave me a compliment that I treasure. It was unexpected and greatly appreciated.

I WROTE A BOOK

I wrote a book! I never thought I could do that. The enjoyment people have expressed to me after reading my book has been so much fun.

I wrote the book because of encouragement from a man and his author-wife who had a booth at a community fair. She critiqued it a couple times, a great help, and his company published the book. In early June 2004, eighteen months after <u>Home Run</u> was published, all costs for 500 copies were recovered with $142.00 extra.

Before writing the book, I went to the vicinity, drove around the area taking pictures, talked with a ranger, and took notes as I listened to information Viola Winschell told me. I stayed with her two nights. She and her husband had owned a ranch by Caribou Mountain.

My desire to write the book began when my uncle gave me a copy of his journal before he died. My favorite part was when he was sixteen years old in 1917. He needed to help his Pa and uncle take the huge herd of sheep to the Caribou Mountain summer range located some distance from Soda Springs, Idaho near the Wyoming border.

Alma didn't complain about the work, but he was anxious to get the job done in time to ride his prize sorrel filly back sixty-five miles to the valley (Idaho Fall- Ucon) over a lonely dirt trail with woodchuck potholes and who knows what else. He just HAD to get back in time to play second baseman with his team in the Fourth of July celebration, the biggest event of the year.

The afternoon of July 4th, his team would play the rival community's team that had been champions for the previous four years. They were a snooty bunch, and they had bragged all winter they would be the winners again. Alma and his team just had to beat them. "We can do it if I can get back in time," Alma kept saying to himself.

I admire my uncle. He did his chores without whining, he was kind to people and animals, and he had a goal he would do whatever was necessary to accomplish. And that meant riding two different horses one hundred miles in less than 24 hours. Their camp was not set up until the evening of July 2nd. His Pa needed Alma to take two pack animals to Brockton the next morning to get 400 pounds of salt for the sheep. Then he could leave for the Valley.

In spite of some real challenges on the trail, Alma did make it in time to play with his team. At the end of the ninth inning, both teams were tied. A tenth inning began. The rival team struck out. When it was Alma's turn to bat, he had two strikes and then the ball connected and flew clear out of the ball park. Alma's team won the game by two runs. Hooray! Hooray!

DIRECTING THE MASTER SINGERS

The recital at the tabernacle went well. The president of the Master Singers in St. George, Utah told me afterwards, "When we look into your eyes and the expression on your face, we sing beyond our ability; there is something about you." It was good for me to feel the pure love and respect coming from that group of men at every rehearsal and performance. We performed 12 programs that season of 2000-2001.

In St. George, I sang with the Southwest Symphonic Chorale the four years I lived there. We performed the *Messiah* and other concerts. I had called for an audition and was put through to talk with the director. He was very friendly when telling me of his musical training. When he mentioned Wyoming I asked, "Are you from Cowley?" "Yes." I laughed and said, "I'm Elaine Watts. Do you remember me?" We were both shocked!

Ken had been the first vocal student that I gave private vocal lessons to. He was about 13 or 14 years old. It was my first public school job – music K-12, band and chorus. Practically all students in the little town's school system were in my classes. Ken's mother had insisted that I give him private vocal lessons after school, though I tried to tell her I was a piano/organ teacher. Mrs. Peterson replied, "Well, you're the music teacher aren't you?" "Yeah, I guess I am." So I did! Ken received a superior rating at the spring district festival singing Grieg's "I Love Thee." I accompanied him. He has his doctorate, and is a music teacher at Dixie College. He also directed the College-Community Chorale. He announced our relationship more than once. He was an excellent director, and it was great to know I had been part of his development.

In Cowley, I didn't teach the Jr./Sr. high band every day; I got a headache when I did. I gave the town some great programs. I even led the pep band at the basketball games. My Jr./Sr. high school chorus of 45 students took one of the two trophies at the festival in Powell singing a J. S. Bach *Chorale* and Randall Thompson's *Alleluia*

Many of the grade school students played instrumental solos which I accompanied on the piano. They received Excellent or Superior ratings. Gloria, my baby, a second grader, charmed the University of Idaho judge with her clarinet solo *Beautiful Savior*. He put her on his knee.

Dan, my son, who was a sixth grader, took the prize for his trumpet solo, *The Lord's Prayer*. The applause almost raised the roof. We all had a great experience. One lady in Cowley, with tears in her eyes, told me she was shocked when her son said he was playing a solo, I think it was on a cornet, for he had fallen out of a tree some years earlier and hadn't been able to physically do such things. It was a good year for a teacher who had never been in a band or directed a band or chorus. But I did have my college degree teaching certificate, a way with kids, and a love for music. The people were wonderful to us.

The worst blizzard I have ever experienced came on my birthday at the end of March. The schools let out early. I sent my children home. I would come a little later. I almost got lost walking the three blocks through the swirling chunks of snow that blinded me. We had to stuff newspapers all around the front door. The snow was relentless. But the power stayed on, and we were safe.

SURVIVAL TRIP TO GLACIER NATIONAL PARK

    We saw five national parks in eighteen days traveling in a 20 foot RV that got 20 miles to the gallon. The mother of my daughter's neighbor invited me to go with her. We would share expenses. I jumped at the chance to go to Canada. She was a good driver and kept us safe, though she was tricky to get along with. I hardly had time to get dressed in the mornings. She slept in her clothes and when she awoke and wanted to go, we went! A few times I didn't have time to get on clean underwear for stretches of two and a half days. A few times we showered free and swam in pools.

    Glacier National Park was spectacular. We had parking spots to sleep in at the park. While sitting in a lodge gazing out the windows at the gorgeous scenery, I heard a boy, about twelve or thirteen, trying to play *Fur Elise* by Beethoven on the grand piano. He would get to a certain spot, forget what came next, and then start over. After four times I walked over and said, "I'm a piano teacher, can I show you the part you are forgetting?" I did. That triggered his memory, and then he remembered it all.

    A lady standing in the background came forward, thanked me, and asked if I was going to the ranger program. I sat with them. Travis and his parents were from Maryland. We wanted to write to each other. I was living in St. George, Utah. I've received CD's of his piano playing. A year later they called from Las Vegas that they would like to come see me. On Saturday, they took me with them to Cedar Breaks, Bryce Canyon, and Zion's National Park. They treated me to lunch at Bryce Visitor's Center. The next day they came to church with me and then to Sunday dinner at my condo. We are still corresponding. It's fun to hear about and see pictures of Travis.

    My RV hostess drove us up to Banff. The Palace Hotel

bus boys heard a few choice words when we couldn't find a parking place up close. At another big hotel, she couldn't find a way into the hot pool. She gave me the motor home keys and told me that I must stay nearby to open the RV. In fast food lines there was usually something wrong with the food, so she would be given something like ice cream.

  She didn't go into the Cardston temple with me. It was nice of her to wait for me to go. I appreciated that. I thought a lot of my mom who had been born in Cardston. Her half-brother had been in charge of laying the capstone of the beautiful pioneer structure. Every hotel and motel was full because of a convention. We met some very nice people who invited us to stay a couple nights with them because the weather was cold and blustery. I think that saved me from getting pneumonia.

  On the way back, we parked one Saturday night in *The Field of Dreams* ball park in Virginia City, Montana next to the city cemetery. We didn't ask permission; the police had already said we couldn't park on a street. We didn't want to chance hitting a deer driving back on the road to the previous town. It was a good place to sleep, way above the town. No one was partying up there that night. She was very nervous about it, but I slept like a log in spite of the wind rocking the RV. It really was a great trip. I was so glad to see all the beautiful sights. We do live in a beautiful world!

PEARL HARBOR

  The end of September 2000, I visited the Hawaiian islands. Pearl Harbor is on the island of Oahu in the city of Honolulu. I was able to get there by bus. A beautiful mural of the battleship U.S.S. Arizona decorates the wall. The U.S.S. Arizona was sunk in Pearl Harbor.

A shuttle took us out to the memorial built over the sunken ship. I could see the outline of the ship underneath as I walked around. There was a subdued atmosphere – respect and reverence for the lives that were lost in defense of our country and our freedom.

The U.S.S. Arizona has a special significance for me. When I was seven years old, my family, along with another family, took a trip to Los Angeles. The U.S.S. Arizona was docked in the harbor, and we went out on it and walked around. I still remember the sailor who teased me. I liked it.

On December 7th, 1941, the Japanese made a surprise attack on Pearl Harbor. They crippled our Navy. It was the beginning of World War II that eventually took both of my brothers to war.

At the Memorial, I felt reverence for the lives that were lost. I reflected on how fragile life is and how we need to appreciate what we have when we have it. When life is finished, the only things that will truly matter is who we have loved and who loves us. I had the opportunity to be around the Polynesian people. It was a good experience.

MUSIC

Martin Luther said, "Music is a precious gift of God."

In December 2006, my daughter Julie Ann, and her daughter Anisha, made a CD of Christmas songs to give to our family and Julie's friends. I accompanied them on the piano. One of the songs we did was one I had written, "Christmas Carols Take Me to Bethlehem."

Christmas carols take me to Bethlehem.
There baby Jesus was born in a manger.
I stand with the animals gazing on Him,
    the Prince of Peace.

Angels sang, telling of peace on earth.
Shepherds heard their tidings of joy.
They ran to the stable,
    then made known the birth
    of the Prince of Peace.

Wise men came, led by the star so bright,
Bringing their gifts to honor His name.
The carols tell stories of that long time ago,
When Jesus, our Savior, was born.

    I remember that during the Christmas season of 2008 I had been driving around doing errands. As I neared home, one of my favorite Christmas songs, "O Holy Night" was sung on the car radio. It touched my heart so, that when I arrived home, before leaving the car, I bowed my head and thanked my Lord for beautiful music.

    Music, my joy,
        An inner world,
            Unique adventures,
                Companions and retreat

    Illusive, yet tangible
        Emotions reach
            heights and depths
                seeking release

Sparkling prisms
    Many facets reflect
        with pristine purity
            creativity in effect.

(One of my original poems)

A FEW PUBLIC SCHOOL SUBSTITUTE TEACHING EXPERIENCES

    I'm supposed to be retired, but just call me "perpetual motion." Being around young people keeps me young, and I like the challenges. I've been asked, "Aren't you nervous going to the high schools?" I answer, "No, they are the easiest ones." I also do junior high and middle schools. I only sub an average of two full days a week. I might go more often by taking some half-day elementary school jobs if I haven't filled my quota. I substituted for seven school years in two different communities. I could fill a book telling about all my experiences, but I will only choose these few:

    I was called to a high school for a day. The third period was a study hall for only five or six kids. I was sitting at the desk. With only a few students, I try to say "Hello" to each one as they come in. One nice-looking boy walked in, looked at me and said, "You're our sub today?" I nodded and said, "I am," smiling as usual. "How are you?" His answer was, "I like you better than our teacher." Surprised, I said, "How do you know? You don't even know me. I don't think I've seen you before."

    He answered, "No, but it's the look on your face and the feeling that's coming from you." Another student walked in just then, and neither he nor I said any more to each other. I've thought about that incident, hoping I have made as good an impression on my friends, family, grandchildren, and great grandchildren, to everyone, really.

At another high school, I was called for Special Ed, the severely handicapped. During the morning, my eyes overflowed with tears several times. I thought, 'Our Heavenly Father is very mindful of this handful of students. His angels are surely here' – that being the reason, I believed, that my emotions kept coming to the surface.

As I helped one-on-one a senior-age boy and then a sophomore-age boy with their reading and writing, I could feel their humble appreciation for my help and also their eagerness to accomplish what was outlined for them to do. Other times, watching the manner that two girl student aides and one boy student aide interacted with these students, I noted their kindness and caring of them.

At still another high school, I subbed art classes. I was reminded of all the things my children had made in school and had given to me. At the close of one class, unexpectedly, a husky boy came by my desk and said, "You did great."

I answered, "I did? What for?" He said, "You kept control; we can get out of hand." Then a tall boy behind him said, "You are better than you think you are."

At all the schools I try to insert my values where I appropriately can. For example, at junior high schools I often ask them: "Class, who likes to eat pizza? Would you like to eat it the rest of your life, for every meal?" I have their attention.

I continue, "After awhile, it would get tiresome to not have any other choices, wouldn't it?" They respond. "Well, if you don't try your best to do your work in school through junior high, high school and perhaps college, you will end up not having any choices. I don't think you will want to sling hamburgers at McDonald's all your life, though it is a great part-time job while you are in high school." I pause. " You have to earn the privilege to be able to make choices. Now is the time to do that. Your future is coming. If you do your best all through school, you will have some choices." I remember that one time I did this, you could have heard a pin drop. I think they felt my serious concern for them.

When I went to one elementary school a half day to sub fifth grade, I could hardly believe how good they were. I told them they had been a wonderful class and that I would leave a note to tell their teacher. They were lining up to go to the cafeteria for lunch. A little Mexican girl was staring at me with her heart in her eyes. I noticed that and smiled at her. She ran over to me with her arms out to give me a hug.

At another school I subbed a fourth grade. The students were to write one page in cursive about something of their choice of home, events, etc. and then show me.

A big boy for his age sat next to my teacher's desk and brought me a scant half page. I said, "You need twice as much; sit down and think about it. You can." He said, "I can't think of any more." I said, "Yes, I'm sure you can." Another smaller boy walked by his desk and the larger boy hit him in the back with his fist. The smaller boy started crying. I said, "He shouldn't have done that, but you were out of your seat without permission. Don't cry. Go to your seat and work on your writing."

The big boy sat sulking. I didn't pay any attention. He put his head down on his arms. Students were showing me their writing. Finally, he raised his head, looked me straight in the eye and said aloud, "I think I'll contact my attorney about you."

I didn't reply, thinking, "What can I do to get this boy to cooperate?" Passing out the math sheets, I was short six papers. I said to him, "Please take this; go to the office as fast as you can to get me six more copies." He jumped up, reminding me of a jackrabbit on the prairie, and was gone and back very soon. Then he was my best buddy for the rest of the morning, and he even wrote more on his writing assignment.

I gave a lot of help to the class for their add-and-subtract assignment. Then I read a book to them. Lining up to go to lunch, one little girl came over and whispered, "The last sub we had – a man – chased him right out of the room." Then I asked the class that if they thought I had helped them really well, to raise their hand. They all did.

I didn't leave the room immediately. When I went downstairs to the office, three little girls were standing in the hallway. They all ran over wanting to hug me. When I walked outside to go to my car, more of my little girls ran across the snowy field to give me a hug. Well, so much for subbing schools. I have many cherished memories.

MY LAST DAY BEING A PUBLIC SCHOOL SUBSTITUTE TEACHER

I went to a huge high school in the district to sub Health Education. I greeted each class, then said with a smile, "In only two or three days school will be over for you. I hope you've had a good year and will have a great summer." I continued, "Today is the last day for me to be a substitute teacher. I've averaged two days a week for seven years. I'll miss being around all the students. It helps to keep me young."

In the first class one young man blurted out, "Then why are you quitting? You don't look that old." I smiled bigger, chuckled, and said, "Thank you for those words. They mean a lot to me" – I paused – "because on my next birthday, I'll be eighty years old." I continued, "I've had people ask me if I'm not afraid of high school students." I say, "No, they are the easiest ones." To the class I said,

"But what I *am* afraid of is being knocked down in the halls if I don't move fast enough to get out of the way when I need to." I added, "I've never before told my age at any school." Then I told them what their teacher had outlined for them to do: a test to take, then watch a DVD.

When I give tests in senior or junior high schools, I always say these words before the test is passed out: "Please put everything under your desk. Then I'd like to tell you what I feel about cheating and copying. If you do that, you are admitting you are dumb." Someone might say something like, "Then so and so is dumb." I ignore such remarks and continue, "And if you allow someone else to steal your work, you are double-dumb." I pause, and then say, "If I see anyone doing what should not be done, I will come take away your paper, and you won't get any credit for the test. Students, I want you to know that I don't want to have to do that." My tone of voice is very serious.

The students learn what to expect from me. While I talk, I insist on complete attention. How do I get that? I speak with a pleasant sounding voice, keep a smile on my face, and have a little fun with things I might say, like: "Hold it; it's my turn. Do you need tape on your mouth? I'll see if I can find some." Also, pauses are very effective. This day, in one class, a young man, at the far corner of the room, surrounded by some adoring girls didn't stop talking to listen to me. I looked at him and said, "Do you have a hard time being respectful?" I waited briefly and then said, "Be fair; its my turn." I do try to preserve a student's self-esteem, but I have a job to do. While watching the DVD, he needed another reminder. I said aloud, "Cool dude, will you please cool it?" He was no more trouble the rest of the class. I kept my voice impersonal, and I smiled at him. He probably wondered if "cool dude" was a put-down or a compliment.

At the end of every class I say as students leave, "Have

a good day." If any bother to say as they leave, "You too" or "Thank you" or both, I know I've been an OK sub. Also, compliments are nice. One young man walked by my desk that day and said, "I like your glasses." I replied, "Thank you. I like them too."

To me, teaching school is like being up to bat in a softball game. You need to make quick decisions about how to react to the way the pitcher throws the ball to you. It is challenging, but when you perform well, it can be very gratifying.